THE O ANTIPHONS

Latin and English
with
Gregorian Chant, Old Hymnary
and
Scripture References

HOPE AND LIFE PRESS

First published in 2017 by
HOPE AND LIFE PRESS

The O Antiphons: Latin and English with Gregorian Chant, Old Hymnary and Scripture References

ISBN 978-19814137-8-2

Copyright © 2017 – Hope and Life Press. All rights reserved.
Front cover shows the Root of Jesse icon.

Published by
HOPE AND LIFE PRESS
2312 Chemin Herron #A, Dorval QC, H9S 1C5 Canada; and
P.O. Box 37, East Longmeadow, MA 01028, USA.
http://hopeandlifepress.com
hopeandlifepress@gmail.com

All rights reserved. No part of this work may be reproduced, stored in a retrieval system, or submitted in any form or by any means, electronic, mechanical, photocopying, recording or otherwise, without the prior written permission of the publisher. This book may not be lent, resold, hired out or otherwise disposed of by way of trade in any form of binding or cover other than that in which it is published, without the prior written consent of the publisher.

Printed in the United States of America.

CONTENTS

About the O Antiphons   5
Note

THE O ANTIPHONS: LATIN AND ENGLISH WITH GREGORIAN CHANT AND OLD HYMNARY NOTATIONS

1. *O Sapientia* – December 17   9
2. *O Adonai* – December 18   12
3. *O Radix Jesse* – December 19   15
4. *O Clavis David* – December 20   18
5. *O Oriens* – December 21   21
6. *O Rex Gentium* – December 22   24
7. *O Emmanuel* – December 23   27

Select Hope and Life Press Books   31

Thereby the prophet says that it is of her, who is descended from David and from Abraham, that He is born. For Jesse was a descendant of Abraham, the father of David; the descendant who conceived Christ, the Virgin, is thus become the 'rod'. Moses too worked his miracles before Pharaoh with a rod; and among others too of mankind, the rod is a sign of empire. And the 'Flower' refers to His body, for it was made to bud forth by the Spirit (Saint Irenaeus of Lyons).

About the O Antiphons

The O Antiphons, also known as The Great Antiphons, are *Magnificat* antiphons that are used at Vespers of the last seven days of Advent in the Western Rite of the Catholic Faith. They are also used as the *Alleluia* verses on the same days during Mass. Each antiphon refers to the prophecy of Isaiah in relation to the coming of the Messiah. The title of each antiphon is one of the names of Our Lord, Jesus Christ, and one of His attributes as mentioned in Sacred Scripture.

There are seven antiphons as follows:

1. December 17: O Sapientia (*O Wisdom*)
2. December 18: O Adonai (*O Lord*)
3. December 19: O Radix Jesse (*O Root of Jesse*)
4. December 20: O Clavis David (*O Key of David*)
5. December 21: O Oriens (*O Dayspring*)
6. December 22: O Rex Gentium (*O King of the nations*)
7. December 23: O Emmanuel (*O With Us is God*).

The famous hymn *Veni, Veni Emmanuel* [*O come, O come, Emmanuel*] is a lyrical paraphrase of these antiphons.

Note

The English hymns and accompanying music found herein are from *The Hymnary – A Book of Church Song* by William Cooke and Benjamin Webb (Eds.), originally published in 1872 by Novello, Ewer and Co.

The root is the household of the Jews, the rod is Mary, the Flower of Mary is Christ. She is rightly called a rod, for she is of the royal lineage, of the house and family of David. Her Flower is Christ, Who destroyed the stench of worldly pollution and poured out the fragrance of eternal life. As He Himself said, 'I am a flower of the plain, a lily of the valleys'
(Saint Ambrose of Milan).

Rod of the root of Jesse [Is. 11:1], and flower that blossomed from his stem, O Christ, You have sprung from the Virgin. From the mountain overshadowed by the forest You have come, made flesh from her that knew not wedlock, O God, Who are not formed from matter
(Saint Cosmas of Syria).

1: O Sapientia – December 17

O Wisdom

O Heavenly Wisdom, hear our cry,
Thou Everlasting Son;
Who with the Father, God Most High,
And Holy Ghost, art One.

Ere Thou hadst formed the lower part
Of all the world we see,
Before the heavens were made, Thou art;
And when they fail, shall be.

Ere Thou hadst called mankind Thine Own,
And made them Thy delight,
Thou reignst by the Father's Throne,
Rejoicing in His sight.

Thou mad'st the waters like a robe,
To gird the solid land;
The wandering stars, the firm-fixed globe,
Were formed by Thy Right Hand.

Come, Heavenly Wisdom, from on high,
And give us that we need:
Unloose our ear, unseal our eye,
And make us Thine indeed.

We wait in faith, we wait in prayer,
Until the happy morn
When Thou didst come our flesh to share,
And for our sakes be born.

To God the Father praise be done:
And equal glory be
To Thee, True Wisdom, God the Son,
And Holy Ghost, To Thee.
Amen.

Latin

O Sapientia, quae ex ore Altissimi prodidisti, attingens a fine usque ad finem, fortiter suaviter disponensque omnia: veni ad docendum nos viam prudentiae.

Scripture References

The spirit of the Lord shall rest on Him, the spirit of wisdom and understanding, the spirit of counsel and might, the spirit of knowledge and the fear of the Lord. His delight shall be in the fear of the Lord (Isaiah 11:2-3).

He is wonderful in counsel and excellent in wisdom (Isaiah 28:29).

See also
Wisdom 8:1
Proverbs 8:1-36
John 1:1-5
I Corinthians 1:30.

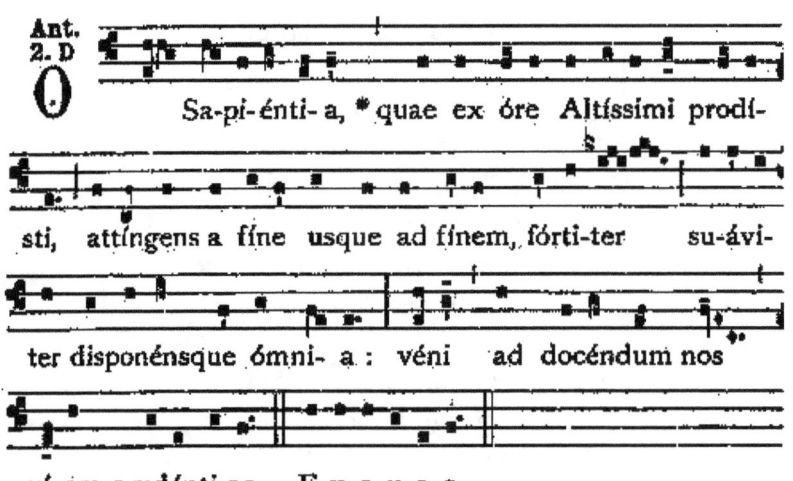

Ant. 2. D

O Sa-pi-énti-a, *quae ex ore Altíssimi prodí-sti, attíngens a fine usque ad finem, fórti-ter su-ávi-ter disponénsque ómni-a : véni ad docéndum nos ví-am prudénti-ae. E u o u a e.

ADVENT.

119

Old Melody.

♩ = 72.

2: O Adonai – December 18

O Lord

O Thou, Who camedst down of old
    To bring salvation nigh,
What time the people of Thy fold
    Sent up a bitter cry:

Thy servant turned aside with awe,
    And that great wonder learnt;
A bush that flamed with fire he saw,
    That yet was never burnt.

When Israel thought all hope was o'er,
    And fear seized every mind,
The Red Sea's wave was stretched before,
    And Pharoah's host behind:

Thou didst not leave them in their need,
    Nor let their prayer be vain;
But didst command Thy winds with speed
    To cleave the waves in twain:

Thy people, like a flock of sheep,
    Passed on, though weak and few;
But Pharoah's chariots in the deep
    Thy Right Hand overthrew.

Come, Saviour, come, and from their foes
    Set free the sons of men;
Our foes are mightier now than those
    That threatened Israel then.

We wait in faith, we wait in prayer,
Until the happy morn
When Thou didst come our flesh to Share,
And for our sakes be born.

To God the Father praise be done;
And equal glory be
To Thee, O Ruler, God the Son,
And Holy Ghost, to Thee.
Amen.

Latin

O Adonai, et Dux domus Israel, qui Moysi in igne flammae rubi apparuisti, et ei in Sina legem dedisti: veni ad redimendum nos in brachio extento.

Scripture References

With righteousness, He shall judge the poor and decide with equity for the meek of the earth. He shall strike the earth with the rod of His mouth and with the breath of His lips He shall kill the wicked. Righteousness shall be the belt around His waist and faithfulness the belt around His loins
(Isaiah 11:4-5).

For the Lord is our judge, the Lord is our ruler, the Lord is our king; He will save us
(Isaiah 33:22).

See also
Exodus 3:2
Micah 6:4
Acts 7:30-31.

3: O Radix Jesse – December 18

O Root of Jesse

O Root of Jesse, Thou on Whom
The Holy Ghost shall rest;
Whose boughs through all the world shall bloom
With healing virtue blest:

True Vine, in Whom we must abide
To bring forth plenteous fruit;
Whose branches, when by tempests tried,
Are firm in Thee their root:

Thou art a shelter from the heat
That burns the thirsty ground:
A hiding place when tempests beat
Upon the plain around.

O Root of Jesse, day by day
To Thee out prayers we send:
Come now, and through the world, we pray,
Thy healing leaves extend.

We wait in faith, we wait in prayer,
Until the happy time
Wherein Thy branches fruit shall bear
Through every distant clime.

To God the Father glory be,
In majesty adored;
To Jesse's Root, the Son; and Thee,
O Holy Ghost; One Lord.
Amen.

Latin

O Radix Jesse, qui stas in signum populorum, super quem continebunt reges os suum, quem gentes deprecabuntur: veni ad liberandum nos, iam noli tardare.

Scripture References

A shoot shall come out from the stock of Jesse and a branch shall grow out of his roots
(Isaiah 11:1).

On that day, the root of Jesse shall stand as a signal to the peoples; the nations shall inquire of Him and His dwelling shall be glorious
(Isaiah 11:10).

See also
Isaiah 52:15
Romans 15:12
Revelation 5:5.

**Ant.
2. D**

O Rá-dix Jésse, * qui stas in signum populórum, super quem continébunt réges os sú- um, quem géntes de- pre-cabúntur : véni ad li-berándum nos, jam nó-li tar- dá-re. E u o u a e.

121 Old Melody.

4: O Clavis David – December 20

O Key of David

O Key of David, hailed by those
In fetters long confined;
For where Thou openest none may close,
Nor where Thou loosest, bind;

Without one ray of light around
To comfort and to cheer,
Poor prisoners we, in fetters bound,
Await Thy drawing near.

Thou, only Thou, canst loose the chain,
Thou only end our woe:
Thou only give us light again,
And let the captives go.

We wait in faith, in prayer we wait,
Until the happy day
When Thou shalt ope our prison-gate,
And call Thine Own away.

From every creature that hath breath
Praise to the Father be;
To Him that hath the keys of death;
And, Holy Ghost, to Thee.
Amen.

Latin

O clavis David, et sceptrum domus Israel: qui aperis, et nemo claudit; claudis, et nemo aperit: veni, et educ vinctum de domo carceris, sedentem in tenebris.

Scripture References

I will place on His shoulder the key of the house of David. He shall open, and no one shall shut. He shall shut and no one shall open
(Isaiah 22:22).

His authority shall grow continually and there shall be endless peace for the throne of David and his kingdom. He will establish and uphold it with justice and with righteousness from this time onwards and for evermore
(Isaiah 9:7).

To open the blind eyes, to bring out the prisoners from the prison, and them that sit in darkness out of the prison house
(Isaiah 42:7).

See also
Isaiah 22:22
Jeremiah 13:13 and 51:19
Matthew 4:16 and 16:19
Luke 1:79
Revelation 3:7.

Ant. 2. D

O Clá-vis Dávid,* et scéptrum dómus Isra-el : qui áperis, et némo cláudit; cláudis, et némo áperit : véni, et éduc vínctum de dómo cárceris, sedéntem in ténebris et úmbra mórtis. E u o u a e.

ADVENT.

122 Old Melody.

♩ = 72.

5: O Oriens – December 21

O Dayspring

O very God of very God,
    And very Light of Light,
Whose feet this earth's dark valley trod,
    That so it might be bright;

Our hopes are weak, our fears are strong,
    Thick darkness blinds our eyes;
Cold is the night, and oh! we long
    That Thou, our Sun, wouldst rise.

And even now, though dull and grey,
    The east is brightening fast,
And kindling to the perfect day,
    That never shall be past.

Oh, guide us till our path is done,
    And we have reached the shore
Where Thou, our Everlasting Sun,
    Art shining evermore.

We wait in faith, and turn our face
    To where the daylight springs,
Till Thou shalt come our gloom to chase,
    With healing on Thy wings.

To God the Father power and might
    Both now and ever be;
To Him That is the Light of Light;
    And, Holy Ghost, to Thee.
    Amen.

Latin

O Oriens, splendor lucis aeternae, et sol iustitiae: veni, et illumina sedentes in tenebris et umbra mortis.

Scripture References

The people who walked in darkness have seen a great light; those who lived in a land of deep darkness, on them light has shined
(Isaiah 9:2).

Then your light will break forth like the dawn and your healing will quickly appear; then your righteousness will go before you and the glory of the Lord will be your rear guard
(Isaiah 58:8).

See also
Isaiah 60:18-20
Luke 1:78-79
John 8:12
Malachi 4:2.

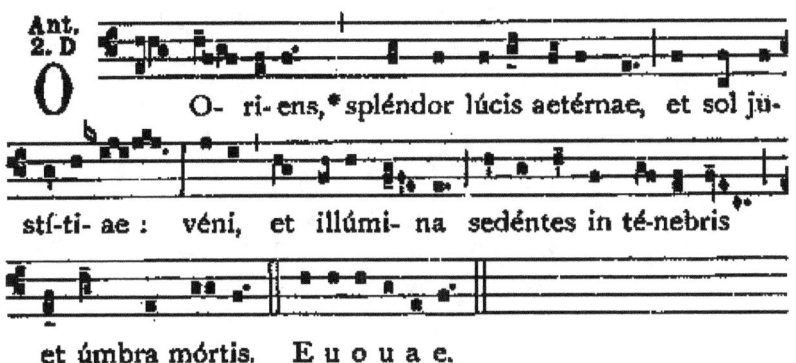

6: O REX GENTIUM – DECEMBER 22

O KING OF THE NATIONS

O Thou, on Whom the nations wait,
And kingdoms far away,
Who midst the Gentiles shall be great,
Whom all men must obey:

Behold the lands where Satan reigns,
Upon his cruel throne;
That sit in darkness and in chains,
And worship wood and stone.

Thine ancient heritage behold,
Thy faithful Abraham's seed;
And join them to the holy Gold
Wherein Thy ransomed feed.

Lead sinners from the paths of sin,
Let scorners hear Thy voice;
And let all heretics come in:
And make Thy Church rejoice!

We wait in faith, we wait in prayer,
Until the happy morn
When Thou didst come our flesh to shae,
And for our sakes be born.

To Thee, the Mighty and the Just,
O Father, glory be;
To Thee, in Whom the isles shall trust;
And, Holy Ghost, to Thee.
Amen.

Latin

O Rex gentium, et desideratus earum, lapisque angularis, qui facis utraque unum: veni, et salva hominem, quem de limo formasti.

Scripture References

For a Child has been born for us, a Son given us; authority rests upon His shoulders and He is named Wonderful Counselor, Mighty God, Everlasting Father, Prince of Peace
(Isaiah 9:6).

He shall judge between the nations and shall arbitrate for many peoples; they shall beat their swords into ploughshares and their spears into pruninghooks. Nation shall not lift up sword against nation, neither shall they learn war anymore
(Isaiah 2:4).

See also
Isaiah 28:16
Revelation 15:3
Psalm 118:22
Haggai 2:8
Daniel 7:14
Jeremiah 10:7
Matthew 21:42
Mark 12:10
Luke 20:17
Acts 4:11
Romans 15:12
Ephesians 2:20
I Peter 2:6.

O Rex génti- um, * et de-siderátus e- árum, lapís-que angu-lá-ris, qui fácis útraque únum: véni, et sálva hóminem, quem de límo formá-sti. E u o u a e.

7: O Emmanuel – December 23

O With Us is God

O Thou, Whose Name is "God with us,"
For Thou with man art One,
And, putting on his flesh, would'st save
His race from exile long;

Not as a King Thou comest now;
No gold Thy throne adorns;
No royal crown is on Thy Head;
Thine is the crown of thorns.

Thou com'st to suffer scorn and pain,
To die upon the tree;
To save Thy people from their sins,
And make us one with Thee.

Oh, make us one with Thee below,
In heart, and will, and love;
And make us, when this life is o'er,
Still one with Thee above.

We wait in faith, we wait in prayer,
Until the happy morn
When Thou didst come our flesh to share,
And for our sakes be born.

To Thee, from Whom our blessings spring,
O Father, glory be;
Like glory to Immanuel;
And, Holy Ghost, to Thee.
Amen.

Latin

O Emmanuel, Rex et legifer noster, exspectatio gentium, et Salvator earum: veni ad salvandum nos Domine Deus noster.

Scripture References

Therefore, the Lord himself will give you a sign. Look, the young woman is with Child and shall bear a Son, and shall name Him Immanuel (Isaiah 7:14).

See also
Isaiah 8:8
Matthew 1:23
Haggai 2:7
1 Timothy 4:9.

ADVENT.

H. S. Irons.

SELECT HOPE AND LIFE PRESS BOOKS

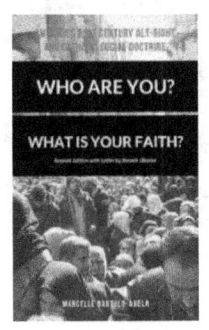

www.ingramcontent.com/pod-product-compliance
Lightning Source LLC
Chambersburg PA
CBHW072116290426
44110CB00014B/1933